The Fire Fetched Down

George Bradley

POEMS

The Fire Fetched Down

Alfred A. Knopf   New York   *1996*

THIS IS A BORZOI BOOK
PUBLISHED BY ALFRED A. KNOPF, INC.

The following publications first printed the following poems:

The New Republic: "The Greenhouse Effect"
The New Yorker: "The Madness of Emperors"
Open City: "Frug Macabre"
The Paris Review: "The Fire Fetched Down," "Museum-Quality Amour,"
     "Nanosecond," "New Age Night at The Nuyorican,"
     "Tobias, or The Idea Whose Time Had Come"
Partisan Review: "The Cliché Made Strange"
Poetry: "Blue That Believes in Nothing"
Western Humanities Review: "A Georgic for Doug Crase," "Opus," "Very Large Array"

"A Short Article or Poem in Response to the Work" first appeared as an essay in an issue of *Verse* devoted to the work of John Ashbery.

"The Fire Fetched Down" was reprinted in *The Best American Poetry, 1994* (Charles Scribner's Sons).

The author thanks the American Academy and Institute of Arts and Letters for its support.

Library of Congress Cataloging-in-Publication Data

Bradley, George, 1953–
    The fire fetched down:poems / by George Bradley.—1st ed.
       p.   cm.
    ISBN 0-679-44620-6
    I. Title.
    PS3552.R227F57   1996   96-4150
    811'.54—dc20   CIP

Manufactured in the United States of America
First Edition

Contents

The Fire Fetched Down

6 × 10 × ∞

See how the hand reaches of its own accord
To take the volume from the shelf, how it lifts
The lid from off that levelled block of reason

And passes through small aperture into a world,
Lifts it like a trap door in the mind and moves
From one life, worn and circumscribed, peculiar,

Into the general life, an immense atmosphere.
Here is no response, simple of the soul, physic
Compound of metaphysics, broken wafer to make us whole.

Aliment is not our element, nor yet antiphony,
And yet mere breath of such an air sets candles
Dancing on the desk to flare on our interior.

Outside, it is any time of day. Outside, night falls.
Engines mutter through the shade, and hours
Rush toward niagaras that are earth's end.

Here, though, distance drifts above a tranquil sea,
And we transform ourselves, become things seen,
Fetching even as starlight, our wink infinite.

I

Frug Macabre

Life, if you're lucky, leaves
something to be desired,
and I do, just fibrillating
for a whiff of old Bordeaux,
as well as hankering after
a huge yet knowing public,
plus enough money to think
about collecting pictures,
plus as much sex as can be
safely fit in this evening
prior to eleven o'clock,
and also dying to learn
all those frantic dances
they don't teach anymore—
the Watusi, the Hully-Gully—
and perform them hours on end
until the bar is exhausted
of strawberries and swaying
cages are lowered to the floor
so exotic creatures in vinyl
may be released to the wild . . .
close your eyes and you almost
see them, the Go-Go girls:
suspended and strictly confined
and thus at liberty to try
about anything, their bodies
not so much moving to music
as forming an integral part,
a flesh and blood harmony
that must be absolute bliss,
or possibly total boredom,
it's hard to be sure which,
even looking past
the ersatz serpentine locks
of their exploding wigs
into the violet faraway

narcosis of their eyes,
and even they don't know,
couldn't tell you the difference,
although doubtless the question
is for them complicated by
the fact that dancers are athletes
and undeep, let's say, or at best
wary of mental agility,
and is it only that reasoning
somehow gets in the way,
sparking rebellions the smart
ones must learn to suppress?
Or is it that thought and action
are irreconcilable enemies
(as Emerson says somewhere,
and he's got lots of somewhere,
you'll have to find it yourself),
the motions of muscle and mind
sapping each other's strength?
And if the two cancel out
(all right, balance each other,
it comes to the same thing),
aren't we forced to adopt
one for our forte by, oh,
forty to have any hope
of doing either one well?
You get a life, and it's body
or soul, pick your poison
(at least that's how it looks
in our culture, though maybe
dervishes view it all differently,
see things sort of homogenized),
which is why your philosopher
kings tend to be slobbering
wrecks, ruins, decrepitudes
drinking, smoking and in general
strafing their cerebellums
until you can't understand
how anything's left upstairs,
much less how they service
whatever gray matter remains,

pump enough oxygen up there
for any ideas to hold out.
But wait, I see a hand raised:
"What about those Greeks,
or Romans, whatever. You know,
healthy minds in likewise
bodies soundly sounding
off in the eternally vernal
groves of academic editions.
Aren't you forgetting the classics?"
Mmmm, well frankly the classics
are insufficiently repressed
to suit our censorious times.
The ancients were incompletely
denatured, because the ancients
were children, even those
than whom we'll never be wiser,
sheer king-of-the-hill,
no-girls-in-the-clubhouse
children, puerile savants
poised on the brink of history
like ski-jumpers at the gate,
their gym-rat culture suffused
with morning light and leading
indices and the tingly feeling
of feeling fine all over.
What did a Greek know
from anxiety? What he knew
was a rock-star ideal of beauty,
brashness, and ego, and I,
for one, am chartreuse with envy,
since self-absorption is strong,
is efficient even as faith
(or one is a form of the other),
and you can write out of ego
as you can out of intellect,
hey, look at Wordsworth,
look at our current conventions
of panic and play in a field
full of blossoming mirrors.
"But it can't be all mere will

to flower. Aren't we meant
in the end to mean something,
to offer the olive branch
of significance, weave a crown
of thorny hope and passionate
despair and nail it down
like nobody's business in
a blood-soaked, final act?"
No harm done if you do,
I guess. But don't you think
it's less than gracious to leave
readers holding the bag?
Besides, people keep meaning
the same things over again:
Gee, it sure is confusing,
How'd we wind up in this mess,
It used to feel much better,
and *Let's just play pretend.*
Give it a few thousand years,
and you can see why our poets
go for that personal touch,
carrying on about childhood
and what was always for dinner
and how Daddy was terribly mean
and Mom was considerably meaner
and both of them up and died
and then everybody died
and now even God has died
and recently even the cat
looks like a trip to the vet.
Curriculum vitae's our version
of vision, confession the stuff
of our dreams, the bottom line
concerning which is anyone
else's bore you to tears.
Not that I blame poets, mind you;
poets are just like people,
wandered waifs, and the past
is the only toy they have.
Still, huddled in the pelting
hailstorm of evocations,

it behooves us to remember
that memory isn't meaning,
it only feels that way,
and instead of clinging steadfast
to our lurid stain, we must
use whatever happened
to impede the skittish moment,
to shatter this agile miracle
and appreciate the pieces:
behold the dust, for instance,
how in time it obliterates
big books and cities, yet
in the short run distinguishes
as nothing else can, profiling
the subtlest bas-relief,
its touch a charcoal rubbing
of the pattern we inhabit;
or consider petroleum products,
how they afflict the Schwarzwald
with brunissure and riddle
Venetian monuments
with a creeping dry rot like
osteoporosis
(sink them, too, in effect;
the tanker channel dredged
through Malamocco agape
to gulp the flooding tide),
and yet how tiny oil slicks
turn rainy streets to rainbows,
taxi drippings to Monets;
and of such spangled raveling
is the fantastic fabric spun,
the web that clings, the wisp
that shreds itself at our hands
(for pinning down our specimen
days isn't easy, butterflies
that they are: I hear
those wanna-be Papas bragging
about meeting life head-on,
and whose life is that sluggish?
Mine's a school of minnows

struck by lightning, a cat-nap
that lost control and woke
weeks later in Shanghai,
a privatized revolution
rioting to overthrow
its sovereign master, me,
bundling me each instant
into its tumbrel, thirsting
to display my severed head,
and after me, my America,
after me, the delusion),
this shot-silk cerement,
the garb by which we grasp
a farouche and cunning myth
that resents our infant instinct
to hold on as best we can
and so thrashes us about
in the sea cave of our days
until we find ourselves
becalmed in later years
and clutching a twilit god,
and that bag of bones is us.
What answer I shall give me
by and by, I wouldn't
know right now, thank you,
nor how to find my way,
but in the errant interim
one's divagation toward
that tête-a-tête may be
recognized in a longing
someone left behind,
the spoor and tell-tale trail
blazed with flash desire,
such as the craving for sex
which, as I said, I'm pretty
much in favor of since
it's every bit as reliable
as heroin addiction and offers
many of the same advantages:
it teaches the value of money,
it keeps you humble, and all

you need is to abstain awhile
to acquire a goal in life,
your existence organized
again around feeling good
as good can be, an achievement
often followed by sleep
(though women do better at this,
maybe men once guarded
the cave, while women curled
up by the fire to snooze,
letting the seed settle in),
not a bad end in itself.
Count on me, then, when
it comes to sex, anytime,
anyplace, up to a point
anyhow, since truth to tell
whoopee isn't everything,
es geht auch ohne, and orgasm
is just like anything else,
tough on a full-time basis.
Need a full-time pastime?
How about looking at pictures?
Call it connoisseurship
and it's even better than sex,
with layers of pornographic,
scopophilic pleasure,
plus the consumer benefit—
here's the clincher—that you
can do it as much as you like.
Do it in public, do it
in private, work in your home
or take the obsessive act
on the road, entering view
after view and pausing there
to absorb what savvy and brio
the artist put into each.
If you like what you see,
why not start a collection?
Come on, it's easy, just look
at the nincompoops doing it!
An eye and some soul are nice,

but all that's really required
is to find Peter, rob him,
and hand the boodle to Paul.
Paul is a gallery owner
and used to such transactions,
and he will send you away
with a world tucked under your arm
which you can tack on a wall
to see if it gets any better
or worse with your attention.
Mere observation can take
a life (and as for the sequel,
I'll believe you exist, Lord
Brahma, provided you let
me come back as a landscape
painter, seeing as painters—
who aren't expected to work
or work out or remain sober
or make coherent conversation
or turn away from nakedness—
live in frigging paradise,
be it ever so paradise *louche),*
or could if lately our artists
hadn't given up painting entirely,
the visual part of the visual
arts usurped in the sixties
by that all too explicable thing,
the concept, and so much so
that one is obliged to fight
suspicions that the object
in objects of art this week
boils down to the cold
calculus and monte bank skill
of dividing *nouveau* from *riche.*
Wonder why poets and painters
don't use the same bars anymore?
Because talking to artists
is worse than talking to actors,
all you get back is the hustle,
and artists now are bullshit
artists, or most of them,

sorry, but there it is.
"Ugh, you poets! A lifetime
spent collecting words
and now you can't find one
good word to say—slamming
dancers, smearing painters,
carving up actors like ham—
as if your own art weren't
the first pretense and last
wormhole of mediocrities!
As if you can call it an art
at all anymore! As if anyone
cared for a poet's opinion!"
Touché, but look at it this way:
we poets have a license
to speak our minds, because
we poets barely exist.
Working a medium *au courant*
as smoke signals, resigned
to book deals as lucrative
as lemonade stands, stuck
teaching creative writing
(all the perks of babysitting
and none of the fan harassment),
ignored, isolated, irritable,
of course a poet will ruin
the party. Explanation
is no excuse, but give
those pouty poetic egos
a movie star's audience
and would they behave any worse?
And where did the audience go?
World population's in meltdown,
so readership goes on respirator?
O Erato, Calliope, who
runs your public relations?
Let's get with it, Ladies,
poetry needs some pub.
So what, it's not understood—
does anyone understand physics?
So what, it's not up-to-date—

isn't cave art trendy these days?
Why shouldn't obscurity create
mystique, antiquity caché?
—But your poetry's not old.
—Older than anyone knows.
—But it's not really old.
—Madame, sad to say,
at a minimum one of us stumbles.
But soft you now, my sorrow,
and hold still while I drown you,
which is harder to do all the time,
and not just because the sorrow
is tougher, better conditioned,
but because the agent of drowning
costs like a month in space.
Priced a good bottle lately?
Whoa, you need a new job!
World population's in meltdown,
and every man jackass
of it lusts for the same
twenty-four ounces that I do,
or at least that's how it seems,
and if I've learned one thing
in life, it's this: the way
it feels is the way it is.
What it feels like, viewed
from cellar level, is payback
time for Tantalus: a market
overflowing with plenty
of expensive mistakes and precious
few bargains, and my shelf empty
of anything other than dreams,
the bottom line about which
is why not indulge to the hilt?
Dreaming won't break the bank.
Care to join me in quaffing
some Château Mouton '45?
Hand on the Bible, I swear
I'd know that wine anywhere,
pick it out in a bomb scare,
sense its beckoning presence

across any room, no matter
how reptile- or mackerel-crowded.
With a deep flush like the glow
of unstained mahogany furniture,
with a dense nose that's compact
of cedar and leaf-mold and tar,
with sediment like snarled string,
like oozy strands of seaweed,
like purple clumps of bark,
taste it once and you'll miss
it forever, speak of it often,
recall it in moments of crisis,
and Bacchus, I'm ready and willing
to believe in you, too—hey,
no problem—if only you grant
I may meet it one day again,
thrill to its kiss in my glass.
And if not? If from here
to senility is a parched slog,
is a prisoner's long walk,
a flagellant's procession?
If all the activity remaining
amounts to a frug in chains
(the Random House unabridged
dictionary, which in holding
a mirror to life has left
something to be desired,
tells us the Frug is similar
to the Twist, and that it is
of uncertain etymology,
perhaps akin to "frig"),
still let us give ourselves
to the dance, yield us to
this macabre conga line
wherein we grasp the pelvis
of the skeleton preceding
and move like waves in the sea,
like wheatfields under wind,
our motion precisely endless,
i.e. to no end except
our strobe-lit bits of clarity,

the flinging shrapnel of ideas,
sensational beliefs such as
the feeling that there is
no worthier ambition than
the Go-Go girl's at midnight,
for when the music stops
this rhythmic agitation
will have been the fun we had,
our impression of a pulsate
passage our only souvenir,
and if dancers know one thing,
if they learn anything in life,
it's what we never shall,
what this immersion was,
what thing this beat has been
that any second goes
gesticulating by,
whether exquisite aria,
"*e lucevan le stelle,*"
or bedrock rock 'n roll,
"sha la, live for today,"
or just some déclassé
country and western sound,
"take me back to Texas"
(Texas? You must be kidding.
There's your proof, nostalgia
builds it's mouse's nest
flat out anywhere,
no matter how scorched or empty,
how sprawling and ill-defined.
Look, the Austin hills,
which any Texan will tell you
are the prettiest part of the state,
might do for a dump in New England.
But OK, what the hell,
Texas, Kamchatka, Tasmania,
take me back anyplace),
"I'm too young to die."
Oh, and speaking of which,
I have a friend in the hospital
in the grip of a serious illness.

He's about my age, and I
keep trying to tell myself
that he ought to see Texas again,
where the gung-ho desolation
is devoutly to be desired.
If you happen to know somebody
big in the cancer business,
could you look into the case?
And if you should receive
reassuring words,
please send them on to me.
I'll print them in this space.

II

AN INVITATION TO JAY CLAYTON

From the land of football recruiting scandals,
Barbeque and kudzu, creation science,
Military schooling and right-to-work laws,
Country of country

Music, come, old friend, to the land of mud-rooms,
Flu, and acid slush, to decaying factory
Towns and autumn foliage fanfare, pilgrim
Mores and pilgrim

Cooking, please come flying. Fly Continental,
If you must, but travel and take advantage
Of the miser's welcome New England offers:
Taciturn greeting,

Shellfish, maple glop, and a local stab at
Wine. Alas, the syrup and wine aren't always
Easy to distinguish, while conversation
Here and about is

Rather less mercurial than the chowder.
We must count on you, then, to keep the table
Lively. Born and bred in the South, where breeding
Matters and manners

Are a sort of spectator sport, by instinct
You will captivate the assorted neighbors
We invite to witness a rare performance,
Charming them silly

With your deep-fried flattery, served in portions
Just this side of fattening, with your gossip
Balanced on the line that divides piquant from
Legal exposure.

Later, dinner done and the others gone or
Gone to bed, we heroes can strive to stave off
Sleep and reminisce for a while, rewriting
Scenes from our epic

College years together, lamenting classmates
Lost or dead, amazing ourselves to notice
Dreams we formed in youth of devoting life to
Language have somehow

Come to pass, albeit in ways we couldn't
Possibly foresee at the time, arrived as
We now are at homes and careers and family,
Come to this present

Peace, or its simulacrum. Jay, what pleasure
Can compare to memories shared upon the
Stroke of midnight? Call it nostalgia, call it
Civilization,

Either way, please visit. It won't be like the
Old days, when the hunger that pounded through our
Veins possessed us, driving us into darkened
Streets toward sunrise.

A SHORT ARTICLE OR POEM IN RESPONSE TO THE WORK

You kept waiting for it to happen all the time. It never did,
    but it would; it was like the sun, endlessly put out.
So many messengers arrived, there was no time to cut off all
    their heads. They would have to do it for themselves.
Everybody was ga-ga about what you were up to: bubbles rose
    among the distorted noses pressed against the glass.
You thought and thought about it until finally nothing needed
    to be done. Then you threw out all the plants.
The orange juice on his Metallica T-shirt served as a kind of
    foil, setting off an enormous penis. Something he
    did before leaving had made a mess on the floor.
    The stain was indelible and spreading, and suddenly
    you realized you loved the little snot to distraction.
Armed with advice from Betty Crocker, she was completely normal
    in a 50's way and an odd choice. She told you
    everything she knew anyhow, and it was what you
    knew, too.
The primrose path at this end of the garden got narrower and
    narrower. Night fell, and it disappeared altogether.
    Then it was set on fire, to be placed among the stars.
They were always worming their way in under the windows and
    around the door, sweet lamentations shaped like
    violin scrolls or the corbels of an overly ornate
    façade.
The melisma of cembalos seemed as intricate as ever, until
    somebody in the audience went absolutely ape and
    you found you had lost the knack of listening to
    the end.
We have reserved a brand new Chevy Blazer, worth $22,000,
    in your name or a toaster-oven, but you must claim
    your prize in person at Heritage Village.
It was pleasant to recall the days of childhood awkwardness,
    before you had been gifted with this fucate fruit
    and forced off toward the horizon.
As if you had set out years ago under a mild sky, only to come
    calling now at this frigid extreme of tundra and

tar-paper shacks . . . a lot could be said about
your entrance into it, a tentative anchorage.
And so once again you were marooned among the mannequins, left
with Volume One of a two volume encyclopaedia and
provisioned with your version of daylight, which
could not help itself and cannot thank you enough.

NEW AGE NIGHT AT THE NUYORICAN

Like I get this phone call from Shirley McClaine,
it's the middle of the night, right,
she's all confused about time,
and she's like how in this previous existence
I was maybe a nomenclator for a forum,
only I was crucified
for incompetence,
which was totally really bogus,
so then I became a logothete in Constantinople,
and I got to wear one of those hats
that look kind of like bandaged volley balls,
but I was way unorthodox,
so they put my eyes out,
you know on purpose,
which was way unempowering,
so then I became a soteriologist
in this library in this monastery in Switzerland,
but there was a problem, sheepskin makes my nose stress,
I was probably already a vegetarian only I didn't know,
and even today I can't eat Swiss cheese,
the holes give me gas,
so anyway I like ran away,
and I got caught and burned on this like stake,
like fondue,
so then I became a cynarchtomachist
in this Renaissance,
it's the stake thing all over again, right,
only it was completely humanocentric,
so instead I become Victorian, an opsimath,
but it just got old,
and all along there were lots of wars,
and I was in them all probably to the max,
and so eventually I moved to New York City,
and then I became a poet
and forgot all the words and hung up.

PAIDEIA

My poems are my children, and I swear
on the graves of my ancestors
I never laid a hand on them,
not even when they exasperated me,
when caring for them left me exhausted
and their cries in the night disturbed my sleep.
I discipline my poems only with hope
of my hard-won approval and the fear
of not being right for this magazine.

My poems are my children, and I have labored
to give them every advantage,
indulging them, up to a point,
and providing the very best education I could.
I let my poems read any book in my library,
even the dirty ones.
I don't worry that they might be privileged.
I worry they might be stupid.

My poems have dared to keep off drugs,
even though they're young
and think they are immortal,
even though, poetry being what it is these days,
the peer pressure to freak out is enormous.
Still, I fret about the company they keep
(audiences these days being what they are);
that's why I implore my poems to be particular,
why I don't mince words
about the facts of life.
My poems are practicing safe sex even as I speak.

Conceived in love and brought into this world
in agony and joy, my poems are my children
and better not call home for cash.
I'm not raising any mama's boys.

It's the mama's-boy becomes the killer nerd,
and I instruct my poems
never to harm anyone with anything but panache.

Semblances and heirs, my poems
will weep when I am dead and confess
things they couldn't tell me to my face:
how they loved me
but were embarrassed by me,
how once they tried to be
like me with small success,
and how in time
they struggled to be other
than I was and couldn't do that, either.

When I am gone and exist only in my poems,
my line shall celebrate my days,
insisting that my acts were brave as any man's,
that my thoughts were complex as another's,
my loves as desperate, as intense.
Adroit, self-confident, and sly,
my poems are my children.
They know how to lie.

TOBIAS, OR *THE IDEA WHOSE TIME HAD COME*

Less bright it was slighter
than your recollection
miniature in fact
the hands upon its breast
withered thin as claws
to see those thread-like lips
it needed all your strength
to think that they pronounced
hosannas once or ever knew
the trumpet's embouchure

so you sat down to mourn
what became a corpse of light
eased it out of samite robes
helped it from its fillet
of crowning artifice
beheld it unembellished
naked of any aura
an echo in the eyes
an aspect of the self
sloughed off like scaley skin

a splendor faded
as if you had believed
dream logic
and now been undeceived
as if a spirit sent to guide
abandoned you instead
parable gone wrong
apocryphal account
tale of a wandered child
but with one little twist

that though you heeded
the strange instructions
found the flashing river

and labored to extract
bright creatures from its side
yet when you strayed
and the effulgence came
to lead you home   O bliss
you knew in grasping
reaching for that hand   its gaze

held something other than
the adoration in your own
contained some composite
of pity and amusement
wit and wistfulness
accustomed as the angel was
to what the light was like
and knowing soon
it would release you
an orphan of the sun

ODE TO ABSENT-MINDEDNESS

Remember that lethargic stream
Of unconsciousness, the freedom from all care
Which limits paradise for academe?
    Banks beset with souls,
   It drifts in eddies over shoals,
Watering seductive meadows where
  It's always August, where the bees
    Hang ever in the air,
    And blossoms never cease;
  Yet among those candid lilies
    And in eternal peace,
The shades remain concupiscent of life,
    Eager every one
To taste a mouthful of oblivion
And so resume our hodiernal strife,
    Forsaking what they've seen
To walk these meadows where the grass is merely green.

  It is the light that calls them back,
For all the dead are given to desire
  Is earth's extravagance of rays:
  The daybreak and ensuing blaze,
The evening sun, the fabled zodiac,
   Or even feeblest fire
  Lit by a momentary match
That flickers to extinction while we watch;
    And though the dead are said
    To have a sun and stars
Unto themselves, yet theirs are not so beautiful,
Perhaps, or ripe with possibility as ours,
  And Elysium is dull
Without the halo that is moonlight shed
    Upon conjecturing,
    Or reflections bred
By iridescence in a insect wing.

With adumbrations as with gaudy shows,
  Light tempts us to mortality,
    As it still beckons me,
Who sometimes linger through a summer afternoon
To see the dilatory shadows prune
     A blowsy damask rose
  Or pollard a catalpa tree;
And gazing on such evidence, I've come to feel
As if the draught intended for my lips
  At birth had somehow missed the mark,
And now, by otherworldly appeal,
  Must be administered in sips
    And on no given schedule,
So that untidy spots, impenetrably dark,
Spatter revery with Lethe's macule,
    And nothingness obtrudes
Its pause for thought in awkward interludes.

  And thus, as if by accident,
Some oversight of inattentive gods,
I find myself the alien inhabitant
  Of countries usually at odds,
The realm of fact, the world of shadow play:
    Conversant with the dead
And yet still shifting for my daily bread,
    Subject to migraines,
  Yet absent-minded for all my pains,
I am everywhere a sort of emigré,
    One whom the border guard
    Inevitably detains
To check the transitory residences
  Declared upon my customs card;
And though fully naturalized in neither
State, who cannot live by bread alone, nor ether,
    I know my way in each
  And shan't be too surprised someday,
Bemused again and stumbling in mid-speech,
    If I come to my senses
    In a familiar land,
  The water running from my hand,
Returned at last to all I meant to say.

III

VERY LARGE ARRAY

Out of the deep and draughty cave of space,
From the far side of the universe, of eternity,
They come—wavelengths, electromagnetic screams—
To this steel Stonehenge of dish-shaped instruments
Orant on three spurs of railroad track displayed
As a gigantic letter "Y" upon our desert floor:
The Very Large Array, composite telescope extending
Into vacuum and incalculable distance, stretching
Into desolation and a vanishing point of scrub.
Persistent whispers, sporadic sighs—the evidence
Exists, for those with ears to hear, in mid-Mojave,
Mid-nowhere, raising in this wide anhydrous Thule
A plein-air glyptotheca, where sparse sage crawls
Away and radio receivers assemble to reflect
Signals somehow in arrival from preternatural remove.
Rhythmic incantations, stabbing shrieks—the oracle
That can't fall silent grows garrulous instead,
Piquing the instinct strong as sex whereby
Stimuli and sense rise to their time-honored rut
And breed conjecture, the earnest shoulder shrugged.
Frantic ululation, protracted moans—the priestess
Speaks as always in ways that beg interpretation,
In hints alluring and appalling and in analysis divine
(Is cosmos vast connection, a spider-webbed abyss?),
In obliquest exegesis, longest possible perspective
(Is all we see meniscus, a bubble blown of stardust?),
Sphingine utterance pronounced in otherworldly waste.
Intermittent murmurs, histrionic howls—the sibyl
Sits among antennae filing off to the horizon,
And there the ancient wisdom is offered us again
In all its classic *ironia*, antique *crudelitas*,
Cryptic observations to be bought at any price,
The running commentary that will not cease
To mock the poverty of our conclusion,
Our spendthift need to know.

NANOSECOND

Someday it must make sense,
This badgering of the past, this fever for a future tense,
Will all add up, although
You'll know by that it's passed from the realm of what we know
Into another kingdom instead;
Somehow the remarkable, if passive, role played by the dead
And tomorrow's heralding
Must merge into conviction, an idea of heirloom quality, a *Ding
An sich* to have and having hold,
And you will grasp the fact that even for the very old
At heart, the object of existence
Is best viewed as an amulet, a token of venerable resistance
To be worn against what aches.
As mutable moons come up, as relentless sunlight breaks
On your dullness like a mood,
Provoking all the natural reactions of rage and gratitude
In all it is enlightening
(Stones throwing gabbroid weight around, vines tightening
Their python grip on a dungheap,
Thoughts rising, swirling, flying like the sparks that leap),
You will believe the braid
Of tangled moments forms a noose you must enter to evade;
Till then, you'll have to live
With something more or less, say with a photographic negative,
With a precisely-drawn
And haloed absence, the outline left by wisdom when it's gone.
For now, this instant is inferno,
A perduring pain, a constant goad permitting you to spare no
Expense in explanation;
Today the nanosecond is your paradise, a minute expectation
Met and met, a never-ending song,
And you're persuaded only that you've never been persuaded long
Or been vouchsafed the key
That might unlock what passes into the great dream of eternity.
Booted off the puffy cloud,
Driven from the smorgasbord of what bliss may be allowed,

What compensation shall we say
Confronts a fractured energumen, awaits the devotee of day?
But there's no way to wish it were:
The implacable myopia has you in thrall, has caught you in its blur,
And the snafu speaks your name;
As you step into its fragrance, your footprints burst into flame.

MESMEROMANIA

Fierce as certain scimitars brandished by a swarm
Of horsemen rampant on the faithless plain, so fierce
And fiercer it must be, as knowledgeable armies
Marching as to war, that slit-eyed incredulity.
As monuments it must impress, must be basilical,
A pillared thing, a pylon, a steepled apprehension;
As altars it must be of stone, adamant misgiving,
Must show its sacrificial smear, its hieratic gouge;
As ceremony grave, as sheer miracle amazing, yet
Pathetic and imploring and as intimate as prayer:
So desperate and so steadfast it will have to be,
Or who will sigh our psalm, who hum our hiemal hymn?
And although an evening thought, a glumness spied
In squinting through the centuries' long light, still
The idea must seem ecstasy, glittering and rapt
Even as the oddball eye, fired as foamy declaration.
This serpent gaze of insight, hypnotic bauble hung
Within the mind as stars are swung across the sky,
Must be for us a madness like the mystery of ages,
Must be, must be, be made to be, or how shall we
Contrive our ordained history, explain away our dreams,
How sing our song in this strange and estranged land,
The inarticulate and sprigless earth to which
We have exiled ourselves?

THE CLICHÉ MADE STRANGE

It must never be a public thing, although
The flourish of its inscription decorate the obelisk,
Though its cadences be trumpeted from parapets, yet
Its inmost note may not be heard except
By inmost ear, a murmur, an insinuation, an aside—
Though its practice be bought and sold, its outward act
A commodity and abundant, still its secret smack
May not be savored save on tremulous occasion,
On midnights amidst a pattering of rain,
On mornings when the chill air is its own chapel—
Except two people meet in earnest, its heart may not be known,
Paramours, communicants, their caresses feeling for
The tenuous integument by which its instinct is expressed—
Except renewed, it may not be, as it is
An imminence, a becoming, and yet an origin,
The only past to which we can in confidence return—
A mood, an imposition, an eccentricity,
The same old story never told the same way twice,
In mind contiguous to mind the spirit manifests
And cannot cease to do so for those who still desire
Its reassuring shiver, its comfort and disturbance,
An ache too intimate for naming, this nuzzling, this nothing,
The subtle commonplace, the table-talk of gods,
All that is most human and all that is most odd.

OPUS

They cut off hands and composed cantatas;
They gutted their neighbors like fish and released
The shape of spirits from bonds of ebony;
They buried populations in pits, seeking the proper word.
They herded women into shivering lines
And raped and stabbed upon convenience.
They burned anything they found susceptible of flame,
Performing that miracle play, *Apocalypse*, every day.
Undaunted, they swallowed the hearts of enemies.
Unmoved, they confirmed dead men in the true faith.
They killed or were killed and always,
Above the smoking city, the vast lake tinged with blood,
There rose a little tune that seemed its own creation,
A lullaby, an anthem, seductive serenade.
Victims, they could be made to suffer—
It was their stock in trade,
Their competence and true possession, the good
They offered, bargaining with fate—
Victims could be broken, equated with the earth,
Starved to shadows and given to the night, and yet
Survivors could not keep from song,
Or never long, would not leave off their burden,
Brave quaver amid ruins.
Melody attended them like misery, because
The bloodlust was the song,
Its sound another kind of killing,
Because the violence and invention were as stops
Along a scale, and it was all a sort of music,
An instinctive rendering, an exuberant attack,
The one coherence snarled enough to answer
In their case: poor connoisseurs of panic,
Their cornered frenzy held the key, and naturally
They could not be restrained or ever end
That common urge and compromised relation,
The uncaring air which they called art
And by which they excused themselves.

AEROLITH

Without a brook to babble, he would never be content,
Wind to whisper, waves that roared, the starry paradigm
Projected overhead . . . except the sun should speak
He could not ever rest in peace. Munch no morsel,
Make no home, he simply couldn't catch his breath, unless
Moonlight were to ask his name, rain reach for his face,
Unless clouds wore fluffy costumes, trees a thin disguise;
Though he yet suspected silence, had lived with his mistake,
Mere air must be moved if he would once be at his ease:
Thunder in its grumblings must intone a dire prediction,
Stones fall from the sky with a modicum of matter.
And if his world be bashful, who but he might take its hand,
Straighten out its stammer, say words it longed to say?
It fell to him to make that effort, to bargain in good faith,
To bring this day his open heart and partial understanding.
Surely one who had the hunger was one could not be shy,
Wherefore he chose conviction, burnished his belief,
Stumbled haply on its presence and made much of accident,
Polishing the remnant, the pitted fragment at his feet,
The inert thing before him that had onetime flown in flames,
Mute survivor of all absence, the extreme of cold and heat,
This dense extrinsic object, for which he could not be blamed.

MUSEUM-QUALITY AMOUR

It didn't want your sympathy and had no need
Of affection, the hot breath of your infatuate regard.
A building razed, a jungle come, river run to dust,
It proved impervious to flattery as to compassion,
Was unimpressed alike by tears and delicate demand.
Evaporated ocean of time already ticked,
Crumbled cenotaph of consummated things,
It could not be won by favor or made to feign concern
For your childlike intentions, the grubby underwear
Of hope, the essential adolescence of the quick.
No one offered up the parchment you embraced,
The mummified panjandrum, the fossilized ideal,
That unflappable decorum wrapped in its waxy sheet
And laid in the sarcophagus of obsolescent days;
The withered cheek you pecked had never been inclined,
Yet you whispered blandishments, nuzzled the deaf ear,
Clutched the granite vacancy, and what choice did you have?
Whose every word was echo, whose very memory was rote,
Your little crush on the grotesque did not admit of cure;
Couched on that rupestral breast, the marble embonpoint
Of hours, you broke your heart for its achievement,
For the *belle dame sans souci,* the unexpectant fact
Which was the past and the way the world appeared,
And which would never love you back.

BLUE THAT BELIEVES IN NOTHING

When the gold light rinsed out of the trees,
Heaping the ground with its residue of sun,
He tried to imagine syllables it wished to say.
Black wood of winter stood against the sky,
A brittle confusion, gaggle of branches,
The snarl at the tip of things,
As he struggled to believe a sere sentence,
In the clatter and click of dry objects,
The patient whispering in the soil.
An obliterating whiteness casually came down,
And he hoped its soft insinuation, flake on flake,
Might speak for him the shibboleth of this world.
But the place he heard never sounded like his own,
Its tongue a dialect he never learned,
Its idiom an alien understanding;
Again and again
The blue that believes in nothing
Pronounced those strange and barbarous words:
Freedom, it said, release, decay.
Leaf and tree and stone.
Earth. Water. Air.

IV

A GEORGIC FOR DOUG CRASE

Anything, Douglas, might take me away from this poor occupation—
Burnt by the sun or half-drowning myself in precipitous cloudbursts,
Breaking the ground till I'm filthy and twisting my muscles in tangles—
Any request, any option, if only the offer were made me.
Given the absence of fame or respect or financial advantage
Found in maintaining a vineyard, restraining its leafy confusion,
Would it surprise you one day to discover I'd thrown it all over?
Gone into real estate? Taken up law or commodities trading?
Who could complain if I scuttled my plans for a plentiful harvest?
Only a fool thinks to live in the castle he builds of tomorrow.
When you perceive that a lifetime is passing and time is against you,
Hoping is difficult work, just as tough as the back-breaking labor
Asked by the vineyard itself, by the seedlings and twisted old rootstocks.
Yet, as the vines often flourish in places where little else prospers,
Due to the soil they prefer, which discourages most cultivation,
Sometimes a man will succeed at a task who is fit for no other.
Over the decades I haven't learned much but this planting and pruning;
That's why I've staked out my acre, arranging the rows in their sequence,
That's why I dream even now of producing a vintage of legend.
    After a lachrimous April has swollen the buds till they're bursting . . .
(Like it or not, I've decided to tell you a little about it,
Bore you a bit, I suppose. Oh, I know it's mundane as a topic,
But the occasions we choose to remark on are always a pretext;
Furthermore, dignified themes carry no guarantee of achievement,
While even ludicrous metaphors work for a talented writer.
Look at the biblical authors, describing their God as a shepherd!
All I can pray is significance creeps in these lines from the edges,
Just as the nutrients leeched from the soil are absorbed across membranes.
Each of us tells what he knows and tells more than he knows in the process.)
    As I was saying, when rain soaks the fields and the weather turns
                                                                balmy,
Sap reawakens the grapevines, ascending through xylem and phloem,
Stirring the blood of those gnarled little men like the sight of young lovers
Itching an octogenarian. Now, if you're lazy, as I am,
Apt to postpone any duty as long as you're possibly able,
Now is the last chance you'll get to prepare for the imminent sprouting.

Cut the vines back! Be severe when you flourish the shears and the
clippers!
It's the resistance that stimulates growth, so you mustn't go lightly.
Leave every plant but a spur and a cane, that's a short branch providing
Fruit in the future and one a bit longer for bearing this summer.
Tie what remains to the stakes, but take care not to strangle your subjects:
Loose but secure's the idea, the way Sterne held the shopkeeper's fingers.
Cuttings in heaps at your feet and the skies passing gently above you,
Sap making sticky work stickier (that's what you get for inertia) . . .
How I should like to be there on the day that you make your beginning!
In our agrarian hours is our paradise truly made earthly.

   Still, as a job well-begun remains only begun notwithstanding,
Surely you won't be astonished to hear how much worry awaits you.
Growing the grape is an art in which nature's the number one culprit:
Insects can swallow your vineyard, the aphids and Japanese beetles;
Black rot and powdery mildew can raisin the immature berries;
Substances deep underground sometimes cause vegetation to wither.
Talk about weather! You'll learn to your sorrow it can't be predicted:
Rain in the proper amount is a rarity verging on fable;
Hail that has come out of nowhere can cancel a season in seconds;
Frost can demolish a vine like the swing of a sharpened machete.
It's a precarious journey that leads from the glass to the gullet,
Yet unimpressive compared to the path from the bud to the bottle.
Work, I'm afraid, is the only thing for it, the rising by morning,
Pulling your boots on, and giving your body to each day's exertion.
Hesiod didn't know much (a mean-spirited man, comprehending
Gods and the dirt, but unwitting of what we may locate between them);
One thing he did understand, though, was life on a farm, about
backaches,
Blisters, and handling a hoe, about harvesting mostly frustration.
Hardship's the name of the game, but there's no point in whining about it;
Learn the first lesson a leaf does and look on the bright side of being.

   Douglas, the branches are sprouting now, eagerly seeking the sunlight.
Each is competing to shade its companions, the way you see piglets
Rooting to reach a sow's belly, or folks at a poetry reading
Shouldering others aside at the bar of the post-mortem party.
Which of the crowd will you cultivate? Now's when to make your decision,
Whether to bear with them all or reduce them at once to essentials;
I would suggest that you get the thing over, to thin out the weaklings,
Those that have never shown promise and won't serve an object hereafter.
(Maybe you misunderstand me? I'm speaking of plants, not of people;

Dining with genius is all very well, but if fools cannot credit
You for a friend, where on earth will you turn when you run out of
                                                            money?
So much for Yeats's disclaimer regarding one's simple affections.)
Only the vigorous growth, then, will merit the time that's demanded;
Otherwise when would you have to be idle? What numinous moments
Passed in surveying the scenery, casting an eye on the cosmos
You have invented at pains, on the leaves as they shrug off the breezes,
Stroked by invisible hands, on the heavens they somehow make brighter?
Sweat is an end in itself, but there's sweetness as well in reflection.
   Don't get too used to it, though, we've a long way to go till we're
                                                            finished.
So much requires your attention that resting is out of the question:
Have you uncovered the base of each vine to increase its aeration?
Have you supported the grapes, so the branches don't break with their
                                                            burden?
Have you been keeping the weeds down? And what about fences for
                                                            wildlife?
Rabbits and deer make a banquet of bark that they strip from your
                                                            seedlings.
Then there's the spray—with the poison you use, you'll outlive
                                                            Mithridates!—
Byleton, Captan, cuprated lime, Malathion and Sevin and Ferbam . . .
All of it's probably carcinogenic, and none of it's lovely
For the environment. Isn't that typical nurturing for you?
Trying to make something grow wants suppressing whatever's around it.
"Let there be light," said Jehovah, by which He meant let there be killing.
Right, then, so here's how to do it. The first thing you'll need is some
                                                            armor:
Search out a surgical mask, or you'll wind up inhaling the vapors;
Put on some coveralls, gloves, and a big floppy hat to protect you
If you're surprised by a shift in the breeze (which reminds me to mention,
Don't pick a day with much wind, or the toxins you aim at a chafer
Will be returned in a puff over you). When you've mixed up your potion
(Pesticide, fungicide, homicide . . .), doing your best not to do in
Pets or the postman by accident, wade through the vineyard, crouching
Under the canopy formed by the leaves to reach subtle concealments,
Those inaccessible spots where the spores are prolific, where vermin
Hide undetected. Now drench down the grapes till they're dripping and
                                                            slather

Every available inch of the vines till the spray puddles up where you're
                                                                    standing.
Soon you will notice your six-legged victims beginning to shudder,
Writhing and dropping to earth, for it doesn't take long to affect them.
Spray on a schedule, spray often, and that's about all there is to it.
Don't spray in June, when the diligent bees pause to pollinate blossoms;
Don't be disheartened by dampness, but rather redouble your efforts;
Don't get dejected if fungus sets in after every precaution:
It's an approximate science, this business of seeking to capture
Sunshine in grapeskins, and poets will tell you the toil is unending.

   Summer's the time when we struggle the most, when a farmer is always
Falling behind in his labors; but then comes the glowing September,
Sweetest of months, when to walk on this planet, aware of the daylight,
Seems a sufficient redress for the problems that plague our existence.
Look at the landscape before you, reflecting the slant rays of autumn—
Yesterday's lingering sorrow, tomorrow's approaching discomfort
(Bodies will ache in this world, it's a nagging you never get used to),
Even the knowledge that your dedication, your skill, and your striving
Add up to nothing (for wine that improves then declines, as the vintage
Also will not last forever, no more than the vines or their owner,
Meaning that each of us tilling our field has been doomed to a lifetime
Spent cultivating a corpse)—how it all disappears in an instant,
Pain and despair, when a rivulet catches your eye, or a treetop
Sways in the wind. The beginning, the end, the oblivious grandeur:
After we cast off the dogma and creed, we are back where we started,
Worshipping what was the primary god, supernatural nature.

   May the enduring divinity Pan choose to aid your endeavors,
Douglas; may molecules speeding through space and the sun also rising
Smile on your projects this day and henceforward. What's more, may
                                                                    whatever
Powers exist, all the forces so dear to the physicist, gather
Over this page; may their energies help in pronouncing this sentence,
Citing those short-sighted criminals, shameless, corrupt and uncaring,
Who have polluted our dwelling, defiled the one avatar ever,
Fouling our nest in a manner an ignorant beast wouldn't think of.
Let's give an aggregate slap-on-the-wrist to our friends in high places,
Fines and community service and homes near atomic reactors
(That, after all, is the great consolation in light of our prospects,
Knowing whoever we blame will be stuck here to share in the fallout).
See the contagion infecting our aquifers, reservoirs, rivers?

Let's hope it seeps into Washington, entering coolers in Congress.
See how the hazardous waste bubbles up from the ground, while the acid
Falls from our atmosphere? Maybe they'll meet in executive lounges,
Causing diseases at Manville and Dow and Dupont. For chastisement
Looms, be assured, a retributive melting, a blast with a vengeance,
Fire that will purify while it annihilates saint with the sinner.
Who dares pretend that we do not deserve it, who have murdered the
                                                    creatures,
Muddied the waters, exchanged a mysterious beauty for eyesores?
Ocean of ages, amen, come to cover the pit we are digging.

   Pardon the passionate outburst, but that's what is called conservation
These days, complaining of practices you in your turn have indulged in.
Anyway, speaking of killing the brutes, here's another dilemma:
How will you keep away birds from the fruits of your summer-long
                                                    contest?
Don't think that something won't need to be done, because birds of a
                                                    feather
Feasting together can empty a vineyard in virtually no time.
Maybe you'll opt for reflective equipment, for clappers and scarecrows?
Birds aren't as dumb as you think, Doug, and none of that's really
                                                    effective.
Shooting them all usually works pretty well, if you're that perseverant.
Cyanide's rather efficient, but birds end up dying around you.
I've got a hunch, though, you're too sentimental for such a solution;
Don't I remember you telling me birdwatching's one of your hobbies?
Well, if a man wants to wander the park in the hours before sunrise
Armed with no more than binoculars, surely it's nobody's business;
Still, the most ravishing plumage and melody can't make them mammals,
Just fluffy reptiles, with allosaur eyes, if you want an opinion.

   All right, so slaughter is out of the question: you'll have to use netting,
Casting an almost invisible mesh over several thousand
Feet and attempting to take in the myriad ramifications,
All the while hoping you don't get too snarled to succeed in imposing
Some sort of order on objects that seem to have other objectives.
Plastic's the netting to use, a material supple yet sturdy.
Sunlight will cause its decay over time, but it's better than cheesecloth;
Cloth tends to tear, and it sags when it's soaked by your spray or by
                                                    rainfall.
Cover the vines in September, and nothing is gained here in waiting:
Fruit still acerbic to you is deliciously sweet to a sparrow.

Lay the interstices loosely (by autumn the grapes have grown tender,
Easily damaged, unlike when unripe) and then gather the dangling
Drapes of the net from between every stake to secure them with
clothespins.
What you are aiming to fashion are tubular chambers completely
Caging the plants, an arrangement resembling elongated larvae
Crawling across the terrain in a scene out of fantasy fiction,
Almost as if you had parodied one pest to fend off another.
   Now come the nerve-racking weeks when you gamble on stretching
the season,
Evenings spent anxiously checking the forecasts for rain (since a downpour
Right at the harvest is worse than no harvest at all, a misfortune
Making for wine so anemic and thin it's no better than water),
Days passed in testing the grapes for their fructose and glycerin levels.
Nature's a practical joker it seems, for a grape with exceptional flavor
Needs to be grown in a region that barely permits maturation.
Vines have to toil to produce a good wine. Their work, too, is not easy:
Difficult soil and unmerciful pruning, a changeable climate,
Herbivores, parasites, mold and disease . . . oh, they're not to be envied!
Never resent them for all they involve, but provide them assistance:
Offer them shelter in winter with snow-fence and windbreaks of burlap,
Help them to weather the frost of the spring and the heat-wave of
summer,
Hold back the harvest a bit to afford them a few extra photons.
   While we delay, is there anything else I've forgotten to tell you?
Let me reflect . . . I'd avoid using mulch, or the mice nest and nibble.
Don't ever irrigate vines, except young ones in drought-like conditions.
Fertilize hardly at all, for to quote Thomas Jefferson, "Frenchmen
Dung very sparingly"—roots that are twenty feet deep have extended
Past your manure, and besides, you'll discover the usual trouble
Isn't a soil that's too weak, but instead one consisting of humus,
Perfect for pickles perhaps, but too heavy and rich for your purpose.
Douglas, the edge of this nation was blessed with remarkable farmland:
Loam that was scraped from a continent during the adamant Ice Age
Since has composed, with the glacial retreat, what we now call Long
Island,
Fertile and flat, an expanse like a prairie adjoining an ocean,
Some of the finest earth ever created, our home and our Eden,
Lost to us now, or almost, nearly buried in buildings and highways,
Covered with asphalt and filled up with cesspools, a wasted potential,
Prime land abandoned to progress while nearby New Yorkers go hungry.

People, of course, are the problem, forever conceiving and getting,
Prone to desire and unable to live without scheming, a species
Covetous in the extreme, the unsatisfied ones, the acquirers.
Which of us doesn't have pipe-dreams of buying a place in the country?
It's hypocritical blaming your neighbor for seeking a pleasure
You have a yen for yourself, yet it pains me to see how we ruin
What we are given—I tell you, one glance at the current construction
Leaves me upset for a week! Ostentation is all it aspires to,
When the attraction out here is simplicity, comfort and function.
Silos are leveled for tennis courts, barns are converted to condos . . .
Farming's a thing of the past in these parts, and what comes to replace it
Doesn't appeal to yours truly, brought up in the old way of living.
Ergo I busy myself with the vines and their ancient requirements:
Others may modernize, I'll plant with Virgil and harvest with Horace.
  Finally the day will arrive when the grapes have attained a perfection,
All of the sweetness the year has to offer subsumed in their rondure.
When you observe that the foliage falls and the branches have started
Hardening up for the cold that's ahead, it's your signal to dig out
Baskets and barrels, to scrub down the press and to hose off the hopper.
Sterilization is what you are after, although you won't ever
Fully achieve it; the goal is to kill off the germs found in nature,
Spores and bacteria normally present, in order to furnish
Yeast with a clear field to work in. The wine-maker's art is promoting
Chemistry leading to wine while inhibiting all that leads elsewhere,
Processes ending in vinegar, sherry, or something like cider.
Just as the grape is attacked on the vine, so the juice runs a gauntlet,
Subject to microbes that prey on it during its riotous ferment;
One little germ running rampant can alter the odor, the reason
Dirty equipment will give you a wine smelling worse than New Jersey.
Sulphur's a good disinfectant—a winemaker's friend is the devil's!—
Some people add it directly, a simple preservative measure,
Dosing the lot to prevent oxidation when racking or bottling;
But an excessive reliance on dosage turns wine into brimstone,
Hot in the nostrils and harsh on the tongue, unattractive though stable.
I say producing a wine is like leading a life, and my motto's
Better to risk real catastrophe rather than settle for safety.
Shoot for the stars, for a liquid ambrosia, the nectar of angels:
Wash your utensils in boiling hot water, then rise with a gentle
Sulphur solution, and that, with some luck, should be barely sufficient.
  Once the equipment is clean, you can ask for some help with the
                                                        harvest.

Gathering grapes is a popular task, so you won't lack for labor:
Friends and acquaintances, passers-by, relatives, relative strangers. . . .
Humans adore making wine, which is why the occasion is festive,
More like a party than anything else, what with laughter and singing,
Good-natured teasing and gossip; a bottle or two from the cellar
Passes alongside the baskets, a taste of the previous vintage
Making light work of the vintage at hand; here's a dog that is chasing
Leaves on the lawn, a woman who chases a child that is clutching
Grapes like a mouse as described by Miss Marianne Moore; now there's
                                                            music
Someone has found on the radio—Saturday's matinee opera!—
Kiri Te Kanawa asks for *ein Glas frisches Wasser,* as picnic
Lunches arrive, and we pause for baguettes with some cheese and a
                                                            sausage.
Douglas, I know very well that you cringe at this sort of performance:
Undemocratic, you say, artificial, elitist, imposing
Silence upon us instead of intriguing our interest; I'll grant you
All of that's true, but you'll have to concede that it's beautiful also.
What is the soul if it isn't inflamed by an ardent soprano,
Doesn't dissolve in the fall of a tenor? Remember how Whitman
Felt that a climaxing aria equalled sublime masturbation?
Voices are surely our ultimate instruments, tuned to our essence,
Part of the body itself, and if nothing's so painful as singers
Searching for pitch, so there's nothing to thrill you like notes from a diva
Wholly controling her art, an experience rarely encountered,
Never forgotten, an intimate moment you needn't feel *triste* for.
    Each to his own way of thinking, of course, and I don't wish to argue.
Shortly the act will conclude, and in time every luncheon is finished;
Then we'll return to the fruit-laden vines, to their mellowing bounty,
Lifting our baskets again, picking up where our reverie left us.
One thing you're right to insist on, however, is never allowing
Social amusements to get in the way of the work that's in progress.
Wine-making wants concentration! You'll sweat as you bend to the
                                                            pressing,
Squint as you eye the sucrometer, sigh as you jot down statistics,
Seeing they're not what you'd hoped for. (I do recommend keeping
                                                            records:
Quantity measured by weight and by volume, the level of sugar,
Date of the harvest, conditions each season, your general comments.
Annals are all that you have to distinguish mistakes made in one year
From the fiasco you make of the next, for inebriants render

Dubious evidence, varying wildly from bottle to bottle,
Changing according to circumstance, mirroring mood and companions;
Memory can't be relied on, of course, an inveterate liar,
Leaving a written account is your one way of gaining perspective,
Notes you preserve as your sum understanding and means of
                                                    improvement.)
    Starting your yeast is the next thing to think about, sparking its courage
So that it froths for the sugar and oxygen more than a stallion
Hungering after a mare—come to think of it, though, even horses
Sometimes need help, and the true tale of animal husbandry, rarely
Told in a poem, would entail rubber gloves and a cast-iron stomach—
Aren't you relieved that we're just making wine? To bring yeast to arousal
All that's required is some fruit-juice and two or three hours by a heater:
Set it aside while you bring in the crop, let it stand while you're heaping
Panniers with grapes; by the time that you need it, the yeast will be ready,
Eager to stir up the must into glutinous bubbles, a turmoil
Asking for room to expand, lest your wine end its days on the floorboards.
    But the dilation to follow can wait for awhile, as we sort through
Each of the bunches to pick out the mold-damaged fruit, a selection
Tedious, tacky, and crucial, since mildew will cause an aroma
Much like a basement in mud time, a fetidness nigh unto fenny;
Culling the yield is a painstaking chore, but you mustn't ignore it.
Would it amuse you, my friend, if I told you a well-guarded secret?
Craftmanship, any and all of it, mostly amounts to the time spent.
Care in the making is what makes the difference, all that demarcates
Wine you'd be honored to drink from the spiritless wash you're so often
Asked to admire, the insipid potations of maladroit workmen
Burdened with pride in themselves but no pride in the art they're abusing,
Plonk, in a word, the ubiquitous trifling, and pray you, avoid it.
Carefully, therefore, distinguish the ripe from the rotten, while loading
Grapes that have met your criteria into the maw of the crusher,
There to be broken before they are pressed, in a step that replaces
Treading in troughs; for the era is past of voluptuous wading
Deep in a sweet-smelling slough with a cloud of irreverent fruit flies
Dancing just out of one's reach. Such a tactile approach is old-fashioned,
Gone with the outhouse and draft horse and plowing undressed in the
                                                    moonlight.
These days the process consists of extruding the fruit through a wringer,
Leaving the seeds, which are bitter, uninjured, but splitting the grapeskins.
Once through the crusher, the pomace goes into the press, to be mangled,
Mashed and compacted, and several times in the bargain; now shoulders

Strain and your fingers contract, because even with mechanization,
Rachets and levers and what not, the pulp offers lots of resistance:
Plenty of muscle is called for to squeeze out the very last oozings!
When you have finished, the matter remaining is totally solid,
Dry as a fossil, a refuse Italians transform into *grappa*,
Adding some water, fermenting the stuff, and distilling the issue.
Some say it isn't so bad once you're used to it, some think it healthful;
I say medicinal use is its only excuse for existing:
Maybe it's good for sedating a cow, or to cauterize bear bites.
Heaven forbid you should drink it, so let's throw what's left in the
                                                        garbage.
    Now that your pail runneth over, it's time for the barrel and air lock.
Cooperage choice is important, contributing much of the fragrance
If you decide to use oak. A suspicion of butter or camphor,
Cinnamon, chocolate, tobacco and leather: the characteristics
Thought to be traits of the wine are in fact merely wooden infusions,
Extract of limousin oak and the tannin it leaves as its trademark.
I like an oaked wine myself, but I know it's a modern-day bias,
No more a part of the grape than the additives known to the ancients,
Flowers and spice they admixed in the draught, or the turpentine favored
Still by the Greeks (it's a pine-resin, really, but smells like it's varnish).
Oak isn't all you can use; Californians have even tried redwood,
Bless their inquisitive souls, with results on the whole unsuccessful,
Curious cordials at best, though perhaps one could learn to endure them.
All wood's expensive, however, and working with wood can be tricky:
Young it's too tannic, and old it's so mild there's no reason to bother.
Steel is an option, though costly, and once I had wine made in plastic
(Quite disagreeable, too, since synthetics impart their own nuance).
Basically, though, you can vinify must in most any container;
Over the years it's been made in ceramic, in stone, even concrete.
Weighing so many alternatives, each with its plus and its minus,
Which will you settle on? Skip every one of them, here's something better:
Glass is the perfect fermenter, you'll find, for it's easy to work with,
Easily cleaned, and will last you a lifetime, despite being fragile.
Gunpowder, paper, the wheel and the word . . . out of all the inventions
Man has been cunning enough to think up, clearly glass was a concept
Second to none, a most human contrivance, our emblem and image,
Sometimes amazingly delicate, sometimes remarkably rugged.
Born in the blaze we have learned to control and that other inferno,
Which we will never subdue, our idea of an alternate order,
Glass is refined from mere sand till it gleams with prismatic effulgence,

Fired to a crystalline beauty and pressed into manifold service:
Lenses for spectacles, telescopes, cameras; panes for the casement;
Tubes for the radio, screens for the tube, and the substance of lightbulbs;
Instruments, ornaments, mirrors and more . . . but its great application,
Nobler than any of these, is that glass makes a glass that's unequalled,
Cradling the wine while revealing its scent and displaying its color,
Foil for the fluid *bijou*, the glyceric and aqueous gemstone.

   Forming the optimal vessel is what endears glass to the vintner,
Coming in various sizes and shapes, nearly all of them widely
Carried and cheap. The fermenter for me is the five-gallon carboy:
Full, it's the largest amount I can lift without regular training.
(Picking the grapes hasn't ended our labor, but only begun it;
This isn't poetry, Doug, and the workers aren't physical shambles!)
Start fermentation by pouring the yeast, which by now should be active,
Into your several jars and then adding the must you've extracted.
Fill the containers no more than halfway at this point, for remember
Yeast reproduction, especially at first, can be violent. Now fasten
Each of the jars with an air lock, an "S"-shaped contraption permitting
Carbon dioxide to force an escape but preventing the entrance,
Fatal to wine, of additional air. It's a question of balance:
Oxygen's needed to drive fermentation (the space you've left over
More than provides enough air for the job), and it's needed in aging
Also, the slow oxidation of tannin resulting in esters
That are the agents of scent; and yet air is a treacherous ally,
Larger amounts of it turning a wine that was amber to umber,
Putting a stop to the perfume and leaving a body that's brittle.
Oh, the *bête noire* of pinot is our bugaboo, too! For consider,
Isn't the basis of life sure to be, soon enough, our undoing?
Even with excellent storage, the air has its way in the long run.

   Let's put that off for awhile and return to the task we're consumed in,
Losing ourselves in its lovely pursuit, for to paraphrase scripture,
Everything else is an emptiness equal to eating an ether.
Now that your carboys are loaded and sealed against air for protection,
Find a location that's quiet and neither too warm nor too chilly.
Fifty degrees is ideal: the containers will percolate smoothly,
Not getting carried away and becoming potential volcanoes.
Sit down and watch for a moment, you might find the process instructive:
Yeast doesn't wait to get on with the business, but leaps to its increase,
Bent on consuming its medium, hot to transform its surroundings,
Rising with energy, just as the grapevines arose from the topsoil;
One or two weeks and the ferment is finished, the alcohol reaching

Ten or eleven percent, even more if the crop was exquisite.
(Most of the wineries add extra sugar to make the wine stronger.
It's an accepted expedient, known as the chaptalization,
But with the passage of time you can tell that a shortcut was taken:
Sugared concoctions taste fine in their youth, but disintegrate later.)
   When the reaction subsides, you can rack the new wine from its
                                                            leavings,
Drawing the murk you have brewed off a layer of disgusting deposit—
Call it the lees or the dregs or the sludge—which comprises the yeast cells,
Most of them dead now their food is consumed, with some vegetable
                                                            tissue,
Plus the occasional insect. If what you're about is a white wine,
Racking may wait if you like, but a red needs immediate action.
White grapes are pressed in advance of fermenting, the way that I've
                                                           outlined;
Red ones, however, are crushed and fermented along with the grapeskins,
Taking on color, and only at this point are pressed for their tannin.
Reds that are left on their lees for too long will refuse to develop,
Harsh from the start and unpleasant well after their fruit is exhausted.
(Frankly, a white wine's for neophytes, easy to make and too easy,
Not to say boring, to drink. Oh, exceptions exist, a few rieslings,
Certain sauternes; but the whites by and large have no gift for maturing,
Won't come around in your cellar, and that, after all, is the object.
White wines don't count, as they say, but the world isn't all to one's
                                                           choosing;
What if you farm an inheritance, given no choice in the matter,
Working a vineyard your grandfather planted to suit his own notions?
What if the climate you live in precludes your varietal fancy?
Here on Long Island, the chardonnay thrives and the diet is seafood:
White wines don't count, I agree, but a white wine is what I'm producing.)
   Once you are racking the wine, the presence of air spells disaster.
Top off the carboys right up to the cork, or you're asking for trouble:
Yeast isn't there to metabolize oxygen, now the initial
Stage is complete, so what air may intrude has the wine at its mercy . . .
Doug, fermentation has ended, but that's not the end of the story.
Sample the wine and you'll find it offensive, a pain on the palate,
Stony, incisive, unyielding, as if you were chewing on granite.
Malic acidity has that effect, but the problem will vanish
Given some time, with the malic transforming itself into lactic,
Which is the acid occurring in milk and a milder component.
(Sorry to lecture—it must seem like alchemy!—a mixture of science,

Guesswork and gobbledegook; but the best way of grasping an art form,
Mauger the mystics, is grasping details, to master the method,
Learn the technique, and ignore inspiration and wonder and instinct.
Learn about what can be taught, for the magic's a mystery regardless.
Knowledge will never insure your success, never fully explain it:
Vinification means trying to bottle proverbial lightning,
Calling for practice and skill, but depending at last on good fortune.)

   Acid conversion takes months to accomplish, a phase that continues
Deep into winter, the air locks releasing the by-products piecemeal,
Sputtering gently throughout frigid nights while you dream of the
                                                           outcome.
After this last agitation is over, the wine can stand idle,
Free to relax, a repose that induces a gradual clearing,
Just as, if left to ourselves, we will pause to collect our impressions.
Filmy precipitates fall from the wine like a heat haze at twilight
(How it delights us in March to envision the dog days of August!)
When the diffusion of moisture and dust imperceptibly settles
Back to the earth as the temperature drops and the birds start to whistle
Songs of the evening. (Then wildlife—a rabbit, two elegant pheasants—
Comes to the edge of the fields to partake of the luminous sunset;
Soon a formation of swan will proceed overhead to the brackish
Waters on which they will slumber, while foxes emerge from their
                                                           burrows,
Owls are alert, and the possum begins its nocturnal excursion.
This is the hour of contentment, more precious by far than the morning.
Last of the day is like last of the wine, a departure to savor.)

   Clarity counts for as much in the cup as it does in complexion,
"Limpid" the compliment prized above all, and that brings us to fining,
Flocculants added in careful proportion to give the wine brilliance.
Fining coagulates particles, changing their ionization
So they attract one another and sink, and the myriad compounds
Used to that end form a litany nearly as odd as the listing,
Found in Rabelais, of Gargantua's search for the ultimate ass-wipe.
Goose necks have yet to be tried, but what *has* been is just as outlandish:
Agars and egg white and every conceivable kind of albumin;
Caseins such as skim milk, and the gelatins triggered by tannin;
Mineral finings like betonite, often combined with some charcoal;
Colloids in viscous variety, proteins in protean numbers. . . .
Finest of finings is blood, though, and best is the blood drawn from cattle.
Ox blood's ideal, but it has to be fresh, which can be inconvenient;
Butchering kine is where I draw the line, so instead I use fish glue,

Known by the trade name of isinglass. Mix it in after a racking,
Wait for a couple of weeks, and the wine will fall bright as the April
Day you decide is the right day for bottling. (A crisp one is called for:
Coolness condenses a haze, whereas warmth puts it back in suspension.)
Siphon the liquid direct from the finings and fill up the bottles
Which you have cleansed in advance with some time in a moderate oven.
Maybe you ought to surrender your principles here, because sulphur
Added in modest amounts can prevent some unpleasant surprises:
Wine that's still working will seep from the cork or explode the container,
Which is a chance that you don't want to take after all you've invested.
Sweat one expends has a way of abridging sublime aspirations;
Better a humble result than have nothing to show for the effort.
    Prior to corking and storage, reserve a few glassfuls for testing.
Check for residual sugar and estimate alcohol content;
Titrate to find out the total acidity, note the specific
Gravity, guess at the glycerin level. But far more important,
Set aside some just to relish. . . . Is any sensation so heady,
Any emotion so grand, as the very first flush of achievement?
Sober assessment can wait till tomorrow—our wine at the moment
Equals the best of Bordeaux (where the classified growths are no longer
Built to respond to a decade of aging and plenty of air time;
All but a few should be drunk by age six and are fading at seven),
Seems to be better than Burgundy (nothing to brag about, sadly,
Now that the standards have crumbled and growers care only for money),
Nearly as fine as a durable Rhône, where tradition still lingers,
Where the Domaine Beaucastel bottles wine to survive generations.
    Stupid comparisons, these, which we really should learn to refrain from.
For the enthusiast, wine isn't ever a matter of ranking,
Never so simple as that; it is only of interest or not so.
What could surpass what we've made with regard to its sheer fascination?
After we've toiled in all weather, perspiring both summer and winter,
Balancing hope against limits imposed by the natural cycle,
How could another's invention appear even half as impressive?
Pass me your glass and I'll pour you some more while we toast our
                                                                creation:
Isn't it worthy of praise? What bouquet, what finesse, what a vintage!
    Here is the poem I have made for you, Douglas, who sent me to study
Classical authors. I give you these lines that have grown as a vineyard,
Reaching fruition through months of hard work, while our president
                                                                thundered
On the Euphrates, delivering payloads when scatterbrained wretches

Starved in our streets without shelter. I leave it to you to pass judgment:
Once you applauded my verse on astronomy—have I succeeded,
Turning to turning the earth, in a field many others have furrowed?
(Heavens to hummocks—apparently Hesiod wasn't so stupid!)
Ours is an art where accomplishment limps in the path of ambition:
Drafts on the page are but pale imitations of words we imagine,
Just as the draught in the glass never matches the wine that we dream of.
I'll be the first to admit that I haven't done all I intended,
Haven't made good on my promise, that great expectations have
mocked me.
Still, in an age when our poets appear to be scared of their shadows,
Maybe this sprawling experiment isn't an absolute failure.
Douglas, I long to read better, so send me whatever you're writing.

A NOTE ABOUT THE AUTHOR

George Bradley is the author of two previous books of verse: *Terms to Be Met* was selected by James Merrill for the Yale Younger Poets Prize in 1985, and *Of the Knowledge of Good and Evil* followed in 1991. While appearing frequently in *The Paris Review*, Bradley has contributed to many other magazines, including *The New Yorker*, *The New Republic*, and *Poetry*. Among the awards his work has received are the Witter Bynner Prize from The American Academy and Institute of Arts and Letters, the Peter I.B. Lavan Award from The Academy of American Poets, and a grant from the National Endowment for the Arts. George Bradley lives in Chester, Connecticut.

A NOTE ON THE TYPE

This book is set in a typeface called Méridien, a classic roman designed by Adrian Frutiger for the French type foundry Deberny et Peignot in 1957. Adrian Frutiger was born in Interlaken, Switzerland, in 1928 and studied type design there and at the Kunstgewerbeschule in Zurich. In 1953 he moved to Paris, where he joined Deberny et Peignot as a member of the design staff. Méridien, as well as his other typeface of world reknown, Univers, was created for the Lumitype photoset machine.

Composition by Graphic Composition, Inc.,
Athens, Georgia
Printed and bound by Quebecor Printing,
Kingsport, Tennessee